DORSET DOG WALKS

BY ROBERT WESTWOOD AND RONNIE

GW00502948

Inspiring Places Publishing
2 Down Lodge Close
Alderholt
Fordingbridge
SP6 3JA

ISBN 978-1-8384668-2-4
Contains Ordnance Survey data © Crown copyright and database right (2011)

Inspiring places

CONTENTS

Maps and "what3words".
The maps of the walks should only be used as a guide, I strongly recommend using OS Explorer maps for detail (also available on bing maps). The relevant map for each walk is indicated.

In some instances I have given "what-3words" details. If you're not familiar with this, it is a sophisticated program that gives a unique three words to every three metre square on the ground. It can be used in conjunction with google or apple maps to give information about where you are in relation to a certain point. The app is free and I recommend having a smartphone also with a free app that gives grid references.

Introduction

If, like me, you've walked dogs for many years, you'll have a good idea what makes an excellent dog walk. Plenty of space to run around safely is important, as well as interesting smells. Perhaps woodland to charge through would come high up your list, depending on the type of dog you walk, and maybe lots of open ground to chase a tennis ball. It's important that we enjoy the walk too, so picturesque places with human interest are always welcome.

The fourteen walks in this book offer a variety of wonderful dog walks in Dorset, a county where over 40% of its area is designated as of outstanding natural beauty. They have been chosen to offer opportunities for dogs of all size and age to run free and also for the enjoyment of the humans they have brought along. Naturally there are places where dogs will need to be on a lead, and there may be cattle and/or sheep in certain locations which will also require a lead. The walks vary in length but none are particularly long or strenuous; information is provided for each.

All of the walks have been tried by my Springer Spaniel Ronnie. He has loved every one and has given his thoughts on their various features. I hope you enjoy any you try as much as we have.

Walk 1 - **Badbury Rings**

This is a fairly short walk at a spectacular Iron Age hillfort, but it can be extended as long as you like by walking around the ramparts.

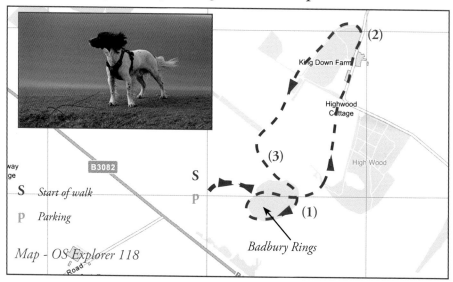

King Down Farm

Highwood Cottage

(2)

(3)

High Wood

B3082

S

P

S   *Start of walk*

P   *Parking*

(1)

Badbury Rings

Map - OS Explorer 118

Road

Notes:

Dogs can run free for much of this walk, apart from around the farmhouse. There are sometimes cattle on the site but often at the southern end.

Dog bins are provided at the start, by the car park, and near the entrance to the hillfort. There are no toilets.

No streams and maybe no water so bring plenty with you, especially if it's a hot day. Some good shady parts though.

The walk:

Start: The National Trust car park at ST960031, nearest postcode BH21 4DZ.

Approx. 3 miles, 4.8km, total ascent about 250ft, 76m.

Go through the gate at the top of the car park and follow the path to your right to the hillfort. Continue through the entrance and go straight over the wooded top of the fort.

Follow the path through the ramparts and head for a gate in the fence (gathering.punks.retire) (1). Go through the gate and turn left along the path. Follow this to where it meets another track and opens out to a farm. You will need to put your dog on a lead for a short while past the farmyard (there are signs to remind you).

Continue straight on past the farm along King Down Drove. There is an ancient oak woodland on your left and near the end of this turn left on a track (author.microfilm.quest) (**2**). Follow this round to the left and along the other side of the woodland.

At the end of the woodland go through a gate (**3**) back on to the site of Badbury Rings. Explore as you wish, walking around the ramparts is easy and enjoyable.

The entrance to the hillfort.

Badbury Rings is an Iron Age hillfort. Probably captured by the Romans in 43CE, although no evidence of a battle or skirmish has been found. Badbury was an important route centre and two Roman roads met here, probably built on earlier tracks. The Romano-British town of Vindocladia was established nearby. The hillfort was abandoned after the Romans came but there has been speculation that it was the site of the battle of Mount Badon where the Britons defeated the invading Saxons around 500CE, led, according to legend, by King Arthur. Many scholars now think it is unlikely to have been the site but there is no doubt it was on an important route west with the once extensive Dorset heathland to the south.

King Down Drove.

For your humans

Easy parking (small fee for non National Trust members). Great views from the ramparts of the hillfort and the wooded centre is a delightful shady spot on hot, sunny days. There are plenty of pubs and cafés in Wimborne or you could try the dog friendly True Lovers Knot in nearby Tarrant Keyneston.

The National Trust's Kingston Lacy (BH21 4EA) is nearby and it's worth noting, perhaps if you're a member, that there is a woodland walk you can take your dog on here. Also near is Keyneston Mill (DT11 9HZ), a botanical garden dedicated to aromatic plants. Dogs are allowed to walk around with you.

Ronnie reckons

A great, varied walk, open space, woodland and the chance to meet other dogs (it's a popular dog walking spot). If you want to improve your fitness you can always charge up and down the ramparts!

You might make a friend.

Looking towards the car park from the hillfort.
Right: My friend Ruby enjoyed it too!

Walk 2 - **A Roman Road**

A walk in a quiet corner of Dorset that follows the best preserved Roman road in southern Britain. Dogs can run free for almost all the route.

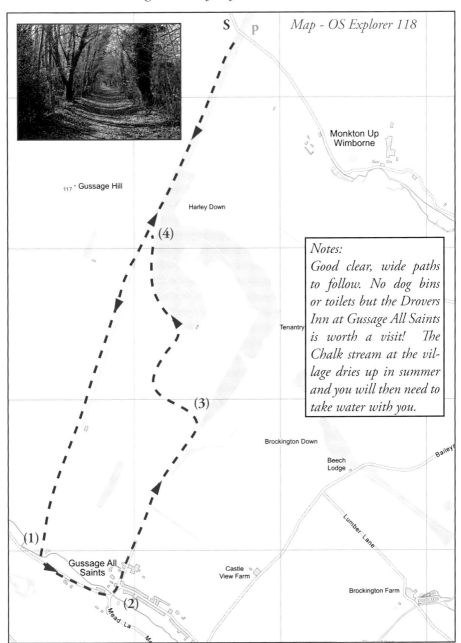

Map - OS Explorer 118

S p

Monkton Up
Wimborne

117 · Gussage Hill

Harley Down

(4)

Tenantry

Notes:
Good clear, wide paths to follow. No dog bins or toilets but the Drovers Inn at Gussage All Saints is worth a visit! The Chalk stream at the village dries up in summer and you will then need to take water with you.

(3)

Brockington Down

Baileys

Beech
Lodge

Lumber Lane

(1)

Gussage All
Saints

Castle
View Farm

Brockington Farm

(2)

Mead La

The walk:

Start: Small parking area on minor road, SU003135, nearest postcode BH21 5NP, (courage.prune.spoiler).

Approx. 5.4 miles, 8.7km, total ascent about 460ft, 130m.

The small road crosses the Roman road, footpath signs lead both north and south along it. Take the path heading south uphill. Follow this all the way to another road near the village of Gussage All Saints – just keep the bank of the old Roman road on your right, you'll not be surprised to learn it is very straight!

Turn left at the road (**1**) and follow it towards Gussage All Saints; there is a chalk stream just before the road which is great for dogs to cool off in, although it is dry most of the summer. As you reach the village take the track by the side of the church (Harley Lane) (**2**), unless you first want to visit the Drovers Inn which is further along the road to the right.

At a junction of tracks keep left (**3**) and then follow this path as it turns right. You will come to a wood where the path turns left; follow this and then keep to the right side of the field with the woods on your right. Go through the gate (**4**) at the end of the field and turn right down the Roman road back to the start.

It really is very straight.

The Ackling Dyke runs for over twenty miles from Badbury Rings to Salisbury and was part of a network of Roman roads joining major centres. From Badbury Rings (see walk page 4) a road would have connected with Hamworthy on Poole Harbour, an important port where supplies arrived. The road sat on a raised bank or "agger" and this is what we see here. Ackling Dyke has a particularly wide agger, perhaps, it has been suggested, designed to impress and intimidate the local population.

Gussage All Saints is a pretty village, the first part of its name deriving from Saxon words which refer to a gushing stream. It is an ancient settlement which archaeologists have discovered sits on the site of an Iron Age chariot factory.

Ronnie reckons

This is one of my favourites; there's so much to explore and usually a few pheasants to chase. Woods to dive into, long grass and wide tracks to run along - this walk has it all! Chalk streams are always good for a dip and you only have to be on the lead for a short section along the road. If they take you to the pub get them to sit in the garden if it's a nice day.

For your humans

Apart from the lovely views and the history, the Drovers Inn in the village is a great, community run pub that welcomes dogs. On a sunny day it has a lovely garden to sit and relax in; plus it's just over half way round the walk. If you wanted you could start the walk from the village, there is space to park by the church, and then visit the pub at the end. The village of Cranborne is nearby with a couple of pubs and people and dogs are welcome to stroll around the Close by the charming manor house.

Walk 3 - **Hod Hill**

Wonderful views for you and your doggy friends, plenty of space to run around, usually firm, dry ground and a stream at the beginning and end if someone needs to cool off.

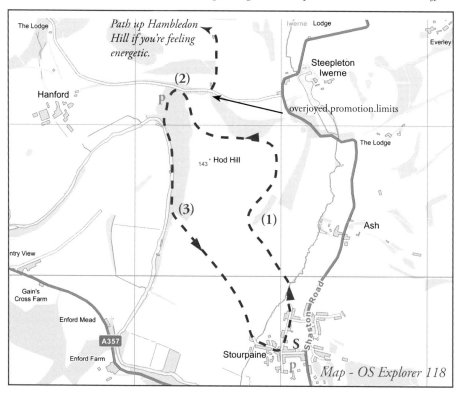

Map - OS Explorer 118

Notes:

Dogs can run free on much of this walk, but please put them on a lead near any livestock; there may be some on Hod Hill.

There is no water on the hill but a stream at the start and end is useful. It's not really possible or advisable to go into the River Stour.

There is a dog bin near the start at the end of Manor Road. There are no toilets on the walk.

The walk:

Start: The northern end of Manor Road in Stourpaine, ST861098, DT11 8QT.

Approx. 2.9 miles, 4.6km, total ascent about 380ft, 116m.

Walk to the end of Manor Road and carry on as it becomes a path. Follow this beside the stream until you come to a junction of paths. Turn left away from the stream and climb the hill towards the hillfort.

Go through the gate (1) and turn right around the top of the ramparts. Continue to the far north-west corner of the hillfort and follow the path down to a small car park at the bottom (2).

Here take a footpath on the left down through the woods; keep going as it follows the course of the River Stour. At ST852103, (backyards.thatched.sped) take the path to your left along Hod Drive (3). Follow this back to Stourpaine, turn left at the end and then left again into Manor Road.

You can of course explore Hod Hill as much as you like; and an alternative would be to start from the small car park at the foot of Hod Hill, ST853112, (butchers.warriors.when), nearest postcode DT11 8PS.

Hod Hill is another ancient Iron Age hillfort with impressive views and mighty ramparts. Possible evidence of a Roman siege has been found; numerous Roman ballista bolts around an Iron Age hut suggested to some that this was a concerted attack on the chieftain, but others have thought it more likely that this was evidence of target practice after the Romans had built a fort of their own on the north-west corner of the hill. Hod Hill is a chalk outlier and looks over the valley of the River Stour to the west and the much narrower valley of the River Iwerne to the east. In early summer it is ablaze with wild flowers. Hambledon Hill is yet another hillfort and also the site of a Neolithic "causewayed camp".

On the ramparts.

Hod Hill, looking towards Hambledon Hill.

For your humans

Wonderful views from this hillfort and neighbouring Hambledon Hill is, if anything, even more spectacular. If you're feeling energetic you could do both; there is a footpath leading up Hambledon near the small car park at the bottom of Hod Hill (see map). For refreshment there is The White Horse in Stourpaine, The Cricketers in Shro- ton and in Child Okeford The Saxon Inn and The Bakers Arms. All are dog friendly.

Ronnie reckons

Another good walk for racing around, plus some woodland to explore. The stream is great for cooling off at the end. A good chance to meet other dogs, but plenty of space if you're not feeling sociable.

Hambledon Hill.

Walk 4 - **Puddletown Forest**

A lovely wooded ramble near Thomas Hardy's cottage, the place he was born and where he wrote Far From the Madding Crowd. The walk starts at Thorncombe Wood Nature Reserve. There are a number of tracks here and in Puddletown Forest. You can make your own route and spend as long as you like; below is the route we took with Ronnie.

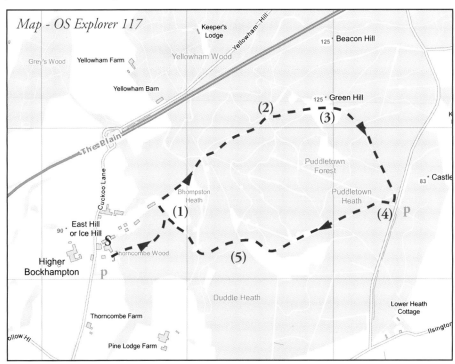

Map - OS Explorer 117

Keeper's Lodge
Yellowham Hill
125 Beacon Hill
Grey's Wood
Yellowham Farm
Yellowham Wood
125 Green Hill
Yellowham Barn
The Blain
(2)
(3)
Cuckoo Lane
Puddletown Forest
83 Castle
Bhompston Heath
Puddletown Heath
(1)
(4) P
East Hill or Ice Hill
90
Thorncombe Wood
(5)
Higher Bockhampton
P
Duddle Heath
Lower Heath Cottage
Thorncombe Farm
Ilsington
ollow Hl
Pine Lodge Farm

Notes:
There are bins at the start and visitor centre. Toilets also at the National Trust Visitor Centre.

Dogs can run free but please note signs; some areas in the nature reserve require dogs on leads during certain times to protect ground nesting birds.

No streams on the route but often lying water - which may be muddy! Mostly good hard paths to follow.

The walk:
Start: The car park at Thorncombe Wood Nature Reserve, SY725921, nearest postcode DT2 8QH.

Approx. 3.3 miles, 5.3km, total ascent about 420ft, 128m.

Take the footpath uphill into the woods at the back of the car park. In a short while turn left on a footpath signed "Hardy's Cottage". Follow the path past the back of the cottage then turn right onto a track signed "Puddletown via Puddletown Forest" (1). At a cross-tracks carry straight on following the blue sign. At the next junction again carry straight on uphill following the blue sign.

At the next junction at SY736931, (factually.receiving.snug) (2) turn right, still following blue sign.

You'll come to a broad track in open woodland, turn left then almost immediately right at a T-junction (3), SY738932, (spots.clenching.salads).

Carry on down this gravel path, as you start going downhill you will see a narrow bridleway on your right, SY741931, (responses.pipe.vowing). Take this and carry on down, ignoring a path on your right.

When you get to the bottom you'll see a road, turn right just before the road and then right again opposite a small car park. Shortly after turn left at a cross-tracks following a path WSW, signed "Roman Road" (4).

Carry straight on at a junction with another path and where the gravel path curves right, keep left on the path leading uphill. At the top of the hill turn right and then almost immediately left through gate and signed "Roman Road Permissive Path" (5).

At the next T-junction turn right past a small pond, through a gate and then turn left signed "Hardy's Cottage". At the cottage turn left signed "Visitor Centre". Follow this back to the visitor centre and the car park.

In Puddletown Forest.

Puddletown Forest was mostly planted between 1924 and 1927. It is managed by Forestry England. The forest is home to rare insects, ground nesting birds such as the woodlark, sand lizards and smooth snakes. There are many tracks so a map is very useful if you're going for a walk there. On the western edge of the forest is Thomas Hardy's cottage owned by the National Trust. It is well worth a visit and in summer the cottage garden is delightful. You will also walk alongside what was one of Britain's first Roman roads, part of the route from London to Exeter. A raised bank marks where the road once was. Look out for swallow holes on the walk, called "swallet holes" on the Ordnance Survey map. These are holes caused by water dissolving the soluble chalk.

It was a lovely, misty morning.

Ronnie reckons

If you're adventurous, then this is the walk for you. Plenty to investigate and great fun charging around the woodland. Maybe not so good if you're a very small dog; but most paths are easy; my friend Ruby the chihuahua enjoyed a walk here.

For your humans

Hardy's cottage is fascinating, a perfect window on rural life in the nineteenth century, and a beautiful garden in summer. The nearby Visitor Centre has a good café. A short distance away is Stinsford Church where Hardy's heart and other members of his family are buried. It's a lovely, peaceful spot and the clear chalk stream beside a footpath behind the church is ideal for cooling off hot dogs, or cleaning up muddy ones!

On the Roman road.

Walk 5 - **Ashmore**

If your dog is energetic and loves chasing through woodland, this is the walk for you. A safe, varied walk along well-marked paths; best done in dry periods but we did it in winter after a rainy spell and it was fine with good walking boots.

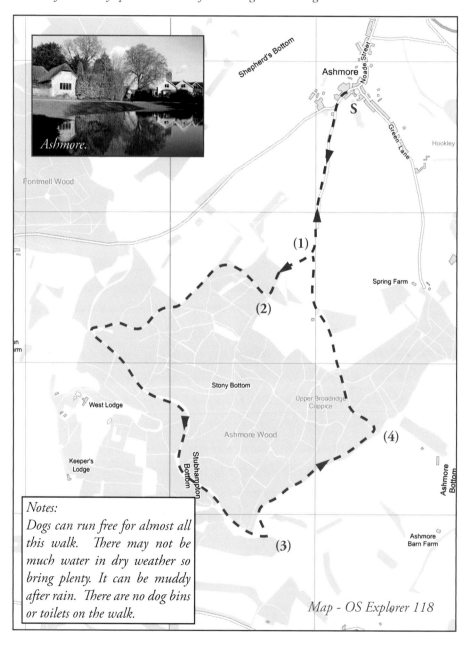

Ashmore.

Shepherd's Bottom

Ashmore

Noade Street

S

Green Lane

Hookley

Fontmell Wood

(1)

Spring Farm

(2)

Stony Bottom

Upper Broadridge Coppice

West Lodge

Ashmore Wood

(4)

Keeper's Lodge

Stubhampton Bottom

Ashmore Bottom

Notes:
Dogs can run free for almost all this walk. There may not be much water in dry weather so bring plenty. It can be muddy after rain. There are no dog bins or toilets on the walk.

(3)

Ashmore Barn Farm

Map - OS Explorer 118

The walk:

Start: The village of Ashmore, street parking is usually available. ST912178, SP5 5AE.

Approx. 5.5 miles, 8.8km, total ascent about 515ft, 156m.

Walk down the road past the church on your right and turn left onto a track (Halfpenny Lane) at ST911177, (biggest.winning.salmon). Continue down this track until you meet a signed footpath on your right at ST909167, (tonic. questions.bulldozer) (**1**).

At a cross-tracks, ST907164, (haunts. triangles.snippets) (**2**), turn right and follow the track through woodland. Follow this as it curves round to the left and go straight on through woodland, following the blue footpath signs. When you have a choice ignore a footpath sign to the right and carry straight on.

You will descend quite a steep slope and arrive at Stubhampton Bottom. Turn left onto the broad track.

Continue down the valley, ignoring the first footpath sign on the left. As you emerge from the woodland at ST906149, (pods.yours.grills), turn left on the path signed "Wessex Ridgeway" (**3**). Follow this with woodland on your left and open fields on your right.

At ST914155 (witless.glove.pines) (**4**) turn left onto the path signed "Ashmore". Follow this all the way back to the start.

Part of the Wessex Ridgeway.

Picturesque Ashmore is Dorset's highest village, situated on top of the Chalk downs. You might wonder why a village so situated has a reliable pond. This might date from Roman times and is a dew pond that is lined with clay to stop it drying out. The village is on an old drove route and the Roman road from Bath to Badbury Rings passes nearby. The Filly Loo festival is held here every year around the summer solstice and celebrates the filling of the pond. It begins with the entrance of the Green Man and involves much dancing around the pond. Visitors are very welcome, but check the website beforehand. Part of the walk uses the Wessex Ridgeway, a 136 mile long distance path, mainly across the Chalk uplands, from Marlborough in Wiltshire to Lyme Regis. The route connects many ancient trade routes.

Ronnie reckons

If you're an active boy or girl like me you won't find a better walk than this. Lots of woodland to explore and race around in and you might find the odd pheasant to put up. Be prepared to get muddy if the weather has been wet.

For your humans

Ashmore is quiet and picturesque; there is no pub or shop but they might enjoy a picnic by the pond. Shaftesbury isn't far and there are plenty of pubs, cafés and shops there. Don't let them go to Compton Abbas Airfield; although it has a very nice café with plenty of interest on the airfield, dogs are not allowed. Likewise nearby Larmer Tree Gardens doesn't allow dogs, the peacocks there aren't very keen on us. Tell them to save both for a trip on their own!

Walk 6 - **Swyre Head**

If you want to enjoy spectacular coastal views but don't want to have to worry about your dog chasing around by a cliff edge (Ronnie's always on a lead there) then try this walk. I'd say it offers the best coastal views in the whole of Dorset, and your dog can run free for much of the time.

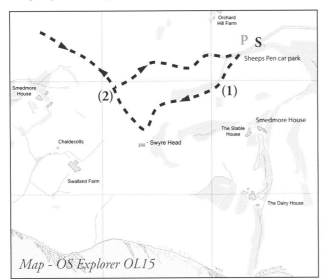

Map - OS Explorer OL15

Notes:
Your dog can run free for much of the walk, although there may be sheep, usually only in one of the fields. There are no dog bins or litter bins and no toilets. There is no water so bring plenty for you and your dog. You can walk from Houns-tout car park in the village of Kingston if you wish, the road is very quiet.

The walk:

Start: Sheeps Pen car park near the village of Kingston, SY943793, nearest postcode BH20 5LL.

Approx. 3.7 miles, 6km, total ascent about 330ft, 100m.

Go through the gate at the back of the car park and follow the path uphill across the field. There may be sheep on the field; if so, keep your dog on a lead.

Go through the gate at the top **(1)** (sniff. photocopy.shameless) and carry straight on with woods on your right, following the path to Swyre Head.

After admiring the view east and west along the Jurasssic Coast, go to the west side of the headland and follow the hedge line northwards, inland. Go through a gate into the next field and continue along the side. At the next gate (Heaven's Gate) **(2)** SY931789 (channel.manager.jousting) go through and carry on following the path along the edge of the field.

I suggest carrying on until the gradient begins to drop away more steeply, then simply retrace your steps to Heaven's Gate. Here, turn left along the path before the gate; this leads back to the car park.

The view west from Swyre Head.

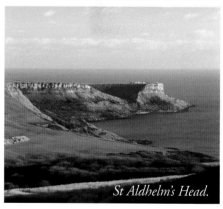

St Aldhelm's Head.

Swyre Head is a promontory on the ridge formed by the Purbeck and Portland limestone and is thought to have been part of the coastline when the sea level was higher. There are great views along the coast towards Kimmeridge to the west and towards St Aldhelm's Head to the east. On the way up you'll have the Encombe Estate on your left sitting in the aptly named 'Golden Bowl'. The Georgian manor is privately owned. To the west of Swyre Head lies the Smedmore Estate. You can catch sight of the elegant Georgian manor from the ridge. Originally owned by the Clavell family, the estate was inherited by the Reverend John Richards in 1817, and it was he who built the folly, Clavell Tower in 1830. The tower is now a holiday apartment run by Landmark Trust and, whilst the house is privately owned, it too can be rented out.

For your humans
A free car park always goes down well. The views are exceptional. It's not far to Corfe Castle and its pubs and cafés, plus dogs are welcome to explore the castle too. You could take them for another walk in Swanage via the famous steam railway. In Kingston is the Scott Arms, where the lovely garden has perhaps the best views of any pub in Dorset, towards Corfe Castle. Dogs are also welcome in the bar area.

Ronnie reckons
A nice, grassy walk for the most part, ideal for those who like to stretch their legs, and good for smaller dogs. Easy to keep an eye on your humans. One downside; no water to cool off in the summer. If your humans insist on going to Corfe Castle you might try to persuade them to give you a walk on Corfe Common, it's another great place for dogs, very safe and excellent for running around.

Corfe Common.

Walk 7 - **Bere Regis**

A ramble on ancient Dorset heathland, criss-crossed by a number of good paths. At the start and finish is a lovely clean chalk stream, ideal for refreshing a (hopefully) tired dog and washing away some of the mud they may have collected!

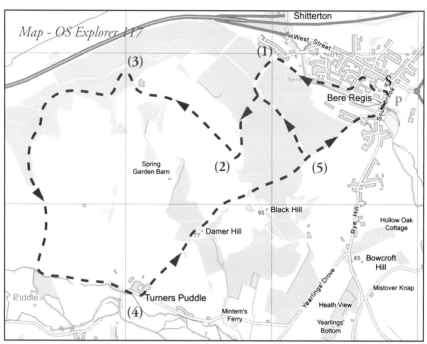

Notes:

The paths on this walk are generally very firm with relatively few muddy patches, even in winter. Dogs can run free for most of the walk, but please be aware of notices. The car park in Bere Regis is free. Dog bins by Bere Stream.

The walk:

Start: Car park, Turberville Road, SY846948, BH20 7HA.

Approx. 5.2 miles, 8.4km, total ascent about 500ft, 152m.

From the car park walk down Manor Road, across Elder Road and into the park by Bere Stream. Turn right and follow the path to the second footbridge you see. Cross this, turn right and at the end of the field go through the gap in the fence and turn left along the path uphill between two hedges (1). Follow this round to the left and shortly turn right uphill signed "Jubilee Trail".

Go through a gate on to "Black Hill Heath" and at the top where another path joins turn right along a broad track (2). At a farm gate (culling.sculpting.paper)carry straight on (the Jubilee Trail turns left). Just past a barn turn left signed "public bridleway" (**3**). Follow path round to the right and then immediately sharp left. (You can stay on the wider path, we found this lower path more interesting and with better views.). Where path divides turn right slightly uphill.

Shortly after turn left by an old hut, then at cross-tracks (quicker.ignore. lemons) turn left heading south. Follow this path down out of the woods and past an old chalk pit.

At the bottom turn left on the track signed "Turners Puddle". Go past the church. There's a ford across the River Piddle on the right which might be a good place for your dog to cool off. Go past the last barn on the left and then turn left on a public bridleway and "Jubilee Trail" (**4**). Follow path round to

the left past the barn and then right, continuing uphill.

Go through a gate and continue straight ahead, past the Devil's Stone at (fulfilled.crumple.fatigued).

When you reach a woodland ignore a path to your right and go straight through the woods to a field at the bottom. In the left corner of the field you will see a gate signed "Hardy Way" and bridleway. Follow this by the side of the field.

Shortly take the wide path on the left (**5**) which will take you back to the village of Shitterton and the path by the Bere Stream which you can follow back to the start. Or you can carry straight on to the road and make your way back to the start via Elder Road – perhaps having a look at the church on the way.

View over Bere Regis from Black Hill Heath.

Ronnie reckons
This walk is a belter, heathland to explore, woodland to chase about in and a lovely stream to cool off at the end. You will need quite a bit of stamina if you're going to make the most of it. Try jumping on top of the Devil's Stone – I managed it!

For your humans
Bere Regis has two pubs, the Drax Arms and the Royal Oak, both dog friendly. The town of Wareham is a short drive away with lots of places to eat and drink, including on the charming town quay. You can also walk along the river if you still have energy.

The ancient heathland is Hardy's 'Egdon Heath' and offers splendid views over the surrounding countryside. The Devil's Stone is possibly an old boundary marker from Roman times. Take a look in Bere Regis church; it has a marvellous carved oak roof, donated in 1485 by Cardinal Morton. There are also delightful carvings on the pews and side columns. The church contains the tombs of the Norman Turberville family, on whom Thomas Hardy based his eponymous heroine in *Tess of the D'Urbervilles*.

The woodland under development between Bere Regis and the heathland is the project of Queen guitarist Brian May, who bought the land with the aim of developing a natural woodland with thriving natural wildlife. It's perhaps no surprise that this is such a dog friendly place!

Bere Regis church.

Walk 8 - **Sturminster Newton**

A picturesque walk along the Stour Valley Way, including the lively market town of Sturminster Newton. Best done in dry weather.

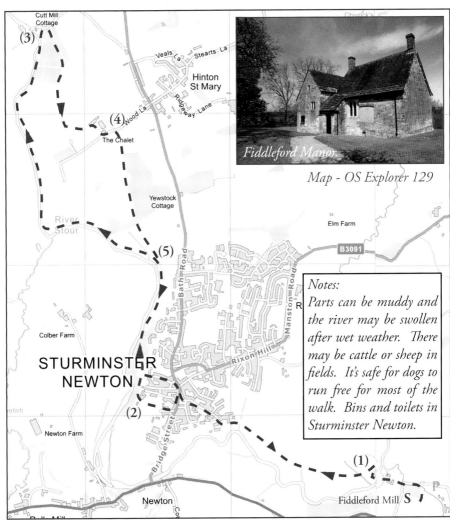

Fiddleford Manor.

Map - OS Explorer 129

Notes:
Parts can be muddy and the river may be swollen after wet weather. There may be cattle or sheep in fields. It's safe for dogs to run free for most of the walk. Bins and toilets in Sturminster Newton.

The walk:

Start: Fiddleford Mill (free car park), ST801135, DT10 2BX.

Approx. 7.3 miles. 11.8km, total ascent about 350ft, 106m.

Turn left out of the car park, left along the lane and past the farm. Carry on over the footbridge across the river and follow the river bank on your right. Reaching the old railway line, climb the steps and turn left along it (1). Follow this to Sturminster Newton.

The River Stour.

Walk through the car park, then left along Station Road and at the T-junction turn left following sign to Town Mill and River Stour. Shortly turn right along Ricketts Lane and follow this path down to the river. At the river turn right (2). Follow the "Stour Valley Way" alongside the river.

After a while the path will follow the edge of a coppice and you will shortly reach Cut Mill (3). Turn right along Cut Mill Lane and then shortly turn right along a path signed "Wood Lane" and "Hardy Way".

At the end of the small coppice, turn right and continue along the bridleway (culminate.writers.spout). Carry straight on across the gallops to field corner and then, keeping the field boundary on your right, turn right just before farm building. Turn left along Wood Lane.

Just after the tarmac road starts turn right along the Hardy Way, signed "Sturminster Newton" (4). Keep close to the coppice on your left and then follow the track as it crosses through the coppice. It is also signed "White Hart Link". Go through the gate at the end of the coppice and cross the field; you will join up with the outward path along the "Stour Valley Way" (5).

Just past the remains of the railway bridge across the river turn left signed "Market Place". This will take you up into "The Row"; follow this to the end, cross the Market Place and at the end of the car park join the path along the old railway line and retrace your steps to the start.

Sturminster Newton sits at an old fording point on the River Stour, which is now crossed by a splendid sixteenth century bridge. A little way upstream from the bridge is the town mill, now a working museum. A mill has been working this spot for over a thousand years. The dialect poet and polymath William Barnes lived in Sturminster Newton, as did Thomas Hardy for several years.

Fiddleford Manor was built in the late fourteenth century, probably for the Sheriff of Somerset and Dorset. It is a charming little manor house, famous for its beautiful roof timbers. It is managed by English Heritage and open to visitors; entry is free.

For your humans

There are plenty of places to eat and drink in Sturminster Newton, many are dog friendly. The Fiddleford Inn near the start of the walk is also dog friendly and has a large beer garden for summer days. You can visit the mill which is just a short walk downstream from where you meet the River Stour at the start of the walk.

Our old Springer Ollie liked a swim!

Ronnie reckons

A great walk! I was off the lead almost all of the time, exploring woods, fields and the river bank. The river has spots where you can safely cool off on a hot day. It's quite a long walk so requires plenty of stamina. You'll probably meet plenty of other dogs on the old railway line, I certainly did!

Walk 9 - The South Dorset Ridgeway

Stunning views across chalk downland and the Dorset coast plus lots of historical interest.

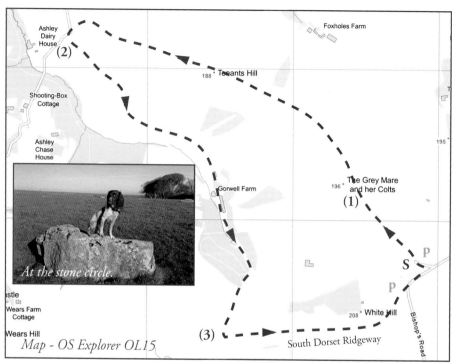

At the stone circle.

Map - OS Explorer OL15

Notes:

There are no bins or toilets on this route. Dogs will be able to run free for much of this walk; you just need to keep a watch out for sheep and cattle nearby. There may not be much water so bring plenty. There's a small stream near Gorwell Farm. After wet weather the first part of the walk can be quite muddy since it is used by farm machinery; maybe best done in dry conditions. However, the Ridgeway is perfect for dogs, plenty of space to run around and firm ground. You can always just walk along this path, perhaps as far as Abbotsbury Castle and back.

The walk:

Start: SY58842 86734, (shorts.petition.steadier), nearest postcode DT2 9HX.

Approx. 4.7 miles. 7.6km, total ascent about 405ft, 123m.

Head north-west along the bridleway (blue marker) also signed "Kingston Russell Stone Circle" and "Grey Mare and her Colts". You will shortly see a footpath signed to the left (1). If you wish to see the 'Grey Mare' take this (over stile), keep the field boundary on your left and then go through a gate on your left. You will see the Neolithic long barrow in front of you.

Return to the main path and continue. After a while you will pass the Kingston Russell Stone Circle on your right, another Neolithic remain. Continue along the path and follow it downhill as it turns left towards Ashely Chase Dairy.

Just before Ashley Chase Dairy (2) turn left onto marked footpath over a stile, SY56473 88228 (sushi.reminds.elbowing). Follow this path; near the top of the field it will curve to the right to a gate at the corner of the field. Then continue along the side of the hill to another gate; go through this and along the track to Gorwell Farm.

Keep on the tarmac road through a small hamlet; as this road bears left take the path on the right uphill signed "Macmillan Way". Keep going uphill through two more gates and following the Macmillan Way.

You will come to the intersection with the South Dorset Ridgeway (3); turn left on this and follow it back to the road near the starting point.

The Fleet from the Ridgeway.

The South Dorset Ridgeway is an ancient trackway along high ground; in this area it is formed from the same golden Jurassic limestone that makes the village of Abbotsbury so attractive. There are ancient remains everywhere, from Bronze Age burial barrows to a Neolithic chambered tomb and stone circle. The views over the coast and the Fleet are magnificent. Elsewhere you will walk over rolling chalk downland with scattered farms and woodland. A great walk for people and dogs!

On the Ridgeway.

Ronnie reckons

A great walk for running; you'll probably meet other dogs along the Ridgeway, it's a popular route for us hounds. Plenty of hedgerows to sniff around in adds to the interest!

For your humans

As well as great views there's lots of historical interest with the Grey Mare and Her Colts Neolithic tomb and the Kingston Russell Stone Circle. Just up the road is the Valley of the Stones Nature Reserve and, of course, Abbotsbury is close by with the Tropical Gardens (dogs are allowed!), the remains of the old abbey and a good choice of places to eat and drink. Dogs are welcome in the Ilchester Arms. It may come as no surprise that dogs are not allowed in the Swannery. Also good fun is a walk (or run) up to St Catherine's Chapel.

The Grey Mare and Her Colts.

Walk 10 - **White Nothe**

Some of the best coastal views in Dorset and a perfect spot for a picnic. Ringstead Bay is nearby with popular, dog friendly beach (all year) and a café.

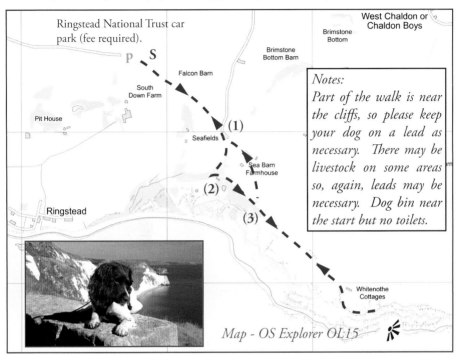

Ringstead National Trust car park (fee required).

P   S

Falcon Barn

South Down Farm

Pit House

Seafields

(1)

Sea Barn Farmhouse

(2)

Ringstead

(3)

West Chaldon or Chaldon Boys

Brimstone Bottom

Brimstone Bottom Barn

Notes:
Part of the walk is near the cliffs, so please keep your dog on a lead as necessary. There may be livestock on some areas so, again, leads may be necessary. Dog bin near the start but no toilets.

Whitenothe Cottages

Map - OS Explorer OL15

The walk:

Start: SY758824, nearest postcode DT2 8NG.

Approx. 3.1 miles, 5km, total ascent about 490ft, 150m.

Follow the track leading from the gate at the end of the parking area. At the bottom, at a junction of tracks (**1**) turn right following sign to Ringstead Bay. A short way down this path is the lovely little wooden church of St Catherine's by the Sea (**2**) (customers.contemplate.renamed). Have a look around if you wish and then retrace your steps a lit-tle way and then turn right by a house, signed "White Nothe". Go through a gate and re-join the coast path. Follow this all the way to the old coastguard cottages visible in the distance. Here take the path to the right towards the old pillbox. Turn left along the path until you reach the stone seat and the wonderful view along the coastline.

When you're ready return to the coast path and retrace your steps. After a gate (**3**) you can keep right across a field past an isolated farmhouse. Go through the gate at the end and back to the start.

The view from White Nothe.

White Nothe is a wonderful 450ft high headland. Stretching out eastwards is a coastline of gleaming white Chalk cliffs providing one of the best coastal viewpoints anywhere on the south coast. To the west is Weymouth Bay and the Isle of Portland. The old coastguard cottages and a precipitous "Smugglers' Path" near the pillbox (don't try it!) give an indication of what went on here in earlier times.

St Catherine's by the Sea.

For your humans

You might have guessed that this walk is one where perhaps more weight has been given to human enjoyment. The views are remarkable, parking easy and a great spot for a picnic. The little wooden church is charming and has lovely engraved glass windows.

Ronnie reckons

There's plenty of interest here and at the start is a huge grassy area for running around and chasing balls. You'll probably see other dogs too. Although you should be on a lead by the cliffs there's still plenty of opportunity to explore off the lead. Be prepared to sit and pretend to enjoy the view over White Nothe, your humans will want to soak it up for a while.

Walk 11 - **Cerne Abbas**

Small but beautiful, this walk around the famous giant rewards with lovely views and an easy path to follow. Finish with a visit to a holy well.

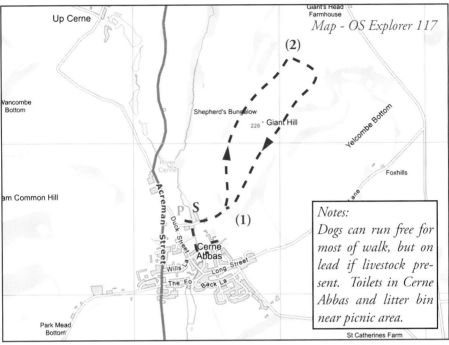

Map - OS Explorer 117

Notes:
Dogs can run free for most of walk, but on lead if livestock present. Toilets in Cerne Abbas and litter bin near picnic area.

The walk:

Start: ST663015, nearest postcode DT2 7GY. Car park and picnic area.

Approx. 2.6 miles, 4.2km, total ascent about 407ft, 124m.

Turn left out of the picnic area and cross the stream. Follow the path as it turns left past a house and then right by a barn. Go through a gate into a wooded area and you will soon see a flight of steps leading uphill **(1)**, signed "Giant Hill". The path leads around the bottom of the fenced field where the giant sits.

Follow the path as it curves around and up the hillside. At the top you will see a stile and signpost (2). Turn right signed "Cerne Giant". When you come to a junction with another path turn right and follow the path downhill towards the earthworks near the top of the giant. Carry on down with the fence on your left and rejoin the path in the woodland at the bottom.

Follow the path back to the stream near the picnic area and turn left down the path alongside the stream. Just past the playing field turn left along a small path over the stream; ideal for cooling off hot dogs. This leads into Abbey Street. Turn left and just past the pond on the right go through the gate into the churchyard. At the end on the right you will find a short path leading to the Silver Well. You can also visit the Abbot's Porch, signed by the gate (fee requested). Retrace steps to the picnic area and car park.

This is a lovely, fairly short walk but it does involve climbing Giant Hill. However the views are worth it. The Cerne Giant has long been a puzzle to those trying to understand its origin. Once thought to have been cut in ancient times and representing Hercules, others pointed out that there was no reference to it until the eighteenth century and inferred it may have been an unflattering caricature of Oliver Cromwell. However, recent research suggests it dates from between the eighth and twelfth centuries, possibly close to the founding of the abbey in the tenth century. The meagre remains of the abbey are nevertheless charming and well worth a look.

The Abbot's Porch dates from around 1500, thirty nine years before the abbey was 'dissolved' by Henry VIII. Perhaps befitting such an idyllic, secluded spot, it has been suggested that its history was largley uneventful.

While the Giant is the most famous of Cerne's attractions, the Silver Well, associated in legend with St Augustine, but much more likely with the Saxon Saint Edwold, is my favourite. A really special spot we always gave our old Springer Ollie a dip in its 'holy' waters and are convinced it helped him to a good old age!

The Abbot's Porch.

Ronnie reckons
I really enjoyed this walk, an easy path to follow, grassy hillside to run up and down and an interesting bit of woodland at the start and finish. The stream is ideal for cooling off in and having a drink. The walk to the well is ok but bear with them if they want to sit by it for a while.

For your humans
The abbey and Silver Well are must sees, and Cerne itself is a lovely, thriving village with a number of dog friendly pubs and café. If you're a fan of real ale or craft beers then the Cerne Abbas Brewery is the place to stock up.

The Giant.

The Silver Well.

Walk 12 - The Dorset Gap

A lovely walk from a picturesque village following ancient trackways along the Chalk ridge with far reaching views of the Vale of Blackmore. Plenty of space for your dog to run around.

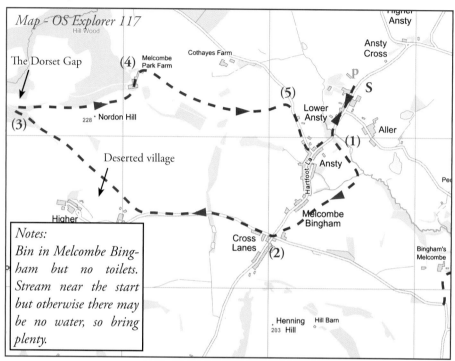

Map - OS Explorer 117

Notes:
Bin in Melcombe Bingham but no toilets. Stream near the start but otherwise there may be no water, so bring plenty.

The walk:

Start: ST765032, nearest postcode DT2 7PN. Small parking area by village hall.

Approx. 3.7 miles, 5.9km, total ascent about 340ft, 104m

Walk southwards down the road. You will shortly see a footpath sign and a gate on your left (**1**). Go through this and follow the path by the side of the stream. Continue, going through another gate, until you come to a footbridge across the stream. Go across and turn right along the path, again by the side of a stream. (It might be muddy just before the bridge.) Continue until you reach another path just before houses; turn right and then shortly left along the road. At a cross-roads turn right along a private road signed "Dorset Gap" (**2**).

Continue along this tarmac road, past a small brick building on the left until you come to a junction just before the buildings of Higher Melcombe. The signpost was down when I was there but take the wide path heading roughly north-west with a field boundary on the left, passing farm buildings on the left. At a junction take the path signed "Dorset Gap". Continue up to the Dorset Gap (3). Here you will find several paths. When you're ready take the path signed "Bulbarrow" heading roughly east. This is the Wessex Ridgeway. Continue through a gate and then down the side of a field with the boundary on your left. At the bottom turn left and go through the farmyard of Melcombe Park Farm (4). Just past the yard turn right signed "Lower Ansty".

There were crops just starting when we were here and it was best to follow the edge of the field until the wide track became apparent. Go through a gate into the next field and then a double stile and follow the path to Cothayes Drove, a small road (5). Turn right, continue to Ansty and then turn left back to the starting point.

There may be livestock at some points of the walk, and dogs should be on a lead if so.

Looking back at the Dorset Gap.

This is a varied walk with stunning views from the Chalk ridge. The Dorset Gap is a saddle in this ridge and a meeting point for several ancient trackways, including the Wessex Ridgeway. For hundreds of years up until the nineteenth century this was an important transport hub, with goods and animals passing between towns and villages. Medieval strip lynchets can be seen on hillsides, indicative of intensive cultivation. On the way to the Dorset Gap we pass the deserted medieval village of Melcombe Horsey; outlines of some of its buildings can be seen as grassy earthworks. Some original buildings remain, including what was the manor, now a rather nice hotel. Many villages ceased to exist in the fourteenth and fifteenth centuries; the Black Death being just one reason.

For your humans

Just a short distance from Melcombe Bingham is the charmingly named manor of Bingham's Melcombe. This is not open to the public but a footpath leads past to the lovely fourteenth century church and there are several more footpaths you might explore. It is an enchanting spot and worth a visit if you do nothing more than wander down to the church and soak up the atmosphere.

Just up the road from the starting point is The Fox Inn, a very popular pub with a garden and dog friendly bar. Also nearby is the pretty village of Milton Abbas where the Hambro Arms welcomes dogs in the bar area. You can also visit Milton Abbey in the grounds of the private school which was once the manor house of Lord Milton who had the old village and its inhabitants removed away from the vicinity of the house and a new one built; the present village.

Ronnie reckons

Lots of interest and space to run around. Some nice long grass to relax in while humans soak up the views. A little bit of road walking but it's very quiet. You might not meet many other dogs. Quite interesting walking through a farmyard - lots of sights and smells!

The church at Bingham's Melcombe.

Walk 13 - **Stonebarrow**

On National Trust land above Charmouth, there are numerous paths to follow and great walking for humans and dogs. Very popular with dog lovers.

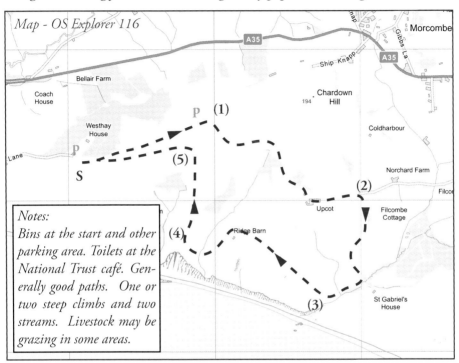

Map - OS Explorer 116

Notes:
Bins at the start and other parking area. Toilets at the National Trust café. Generally good paths. One or two steep climbs and two streams. Livestock may be grazing in some areas.

The walk:
Start: SY382933, nearest postcode DT6 6SD. National Trust car park.

Approx. 3.7 miles, 5.9km, total ascent about 600ft, 183m.

There are many paths you could take and the walk can be altered to suit any preferences; below is the route Ronnie and I took, I specifically wanted to avoid any walking near cliff edges. There may be livestock grazing in some places, in which case dogs should be on a lead. Ronnie was able to run free for almost all the walk when we went.

Follow the track from the first car parking area to the further one. Take the path downhill signed "Chardown Hill and Golden Cap" (**1**). Go through a gate and continue following sign to St Gabriels and Golden Cap. At the bottom of the hill go through a gate and follow path signed "St Gabriel's".

Continue down to Upcot Farm, turn left through the farm and then right at a junction signed "St Gabriel's, Golden Cap" (**2**). When you reach St Gabriel's you may want to continue a short distance uphill to view the ruined chapel.

From St Gabriel's take the path signed "Coast Path", go over a stream and two stiles. Continue to follow the coast path and pink footpath sign "NT 10" (3). At a junction carry straight on following coast path.

St Gabriel's Chapel.

Go into a valley, cross a stream via a footbridge and follow the path uphill. Just past a gate turn right up a side of a field (4). Keep following the path with the hedge on your right. Go over a stile by the gate at the top and turn left (5). Shortly after you meet a wide track take a small path on your right. Follow this back to the car park.

Stonebarrow Hill is part of the National Trust's Golden Cap estate. It sits above Charmouth and the dramatic Jurassic Coast between there and Golden Cap, at 188m or 620ft, the highest point on the south coast. It dominates the view from the hill and, if you wish, can be climbed from St Gabriel's. Be careful with dogs near the cliff edge though. Golden cap is so-called because of its top layer of Cretaceous Greensand. This sits on Lower Jurassic sediments and is part of a feature known as the Great Unconformity. The Middle and Upper Jurassic are missing, these layers having been eroded when the area was land. The sea returned in the Cretaceous Period and deposited more sediments.

The old village of Stanton St Gabriel was once on the old coach road from Dorchester to Exeter. As this suffered from the threat of cliff erosion a new road was built inland (now the A35). The village was abandoned about 200 years ago as villagers left to find work elsewhere. The ruined church was in use until the early nineteenth century; it is said it was used by smugglers to hide contraband before it was distributed inland.

Ronnie reckons

A great place for running around and meeting other dogs. There's wide tracks, grassy areas and hedgerows to explore. It's ideal if you like charging around or if you just want to plod along the paths. A couple of streams are useful for having a drink and cooling off. There's one or two steep climbs so make sure your humans are up to it.

For your humans

As well as enjoying the wonderful views you might find the National Trust café open (check website), The grassy areas are ideal for picnics and in nearby Charmouth The George, The Royal Oak and the Charmouth Fish Bar are all dog friendly. Dogs can run on East Charmouth beach all year (see ' On the Beach'). Lyme Regis is also a short drive away with lots of choice for eating and drinking and dog friendly beaches.

Walk 14 - Lambert's Castle

Two very different Dorset hillforts with lovely views across the Marshwood Vale. Very popular dog walking spot!

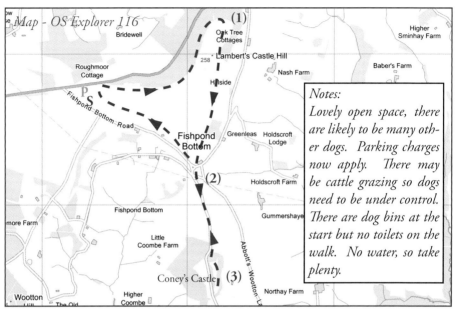

Map - OS Explorer 116

Notes: Lovely open space, there are likely to be many other dogs. Parking charges now apply. There may be cattle grazing so dogs need to be under control. There are dog bins at the start but no toilets on the walk. No water, so take plenty.

The walk:
Start: SY366988, nearest postcode EX13 5UN.

Approx. 2.8 miles, 5km, total ascent about 330ft, 100m.

The walk starts at the National Trust car park. Go through the gate and walk up the hill keeping the tree line to your left. At the top go through the gap in the ramparts of the hillfort and have a wander around here (1). Walk back through the gap and follow the track down the other, eastern, side of the hill. At the south-eastern corner of the hill go through a gate signed "Wessex Ridgeway" and "Liberty Trail" and descend to a road.

Walk carefully down the road and shortly take the left fork (Long Lane) (2). When you reach a small car park (3) go through it and look for a path through woods on the left. This turns into a charming sunken wooded lane and follows the ramparts of the small hillfort that is Coney's Castle. I suggest coming back the same way when you near the road again.

Return along the road to Lambert's Castle Hill. Go back up the path where you exited the hill before and turn left at the top and follow the path on the southern side of the hill back to the car park. You can, of course, wander around the hill as much as you like!

The ramparts at Lambert's Castle.

For your humans

If you're keen on hillforts and the amazing views they provide you could also visit nearby Pilsdon Pen with convenient parking at the bottom (ST41393 00912, sourcing.clubs.flagged, nearest postcode DT6 5NX).

You could just wear your dogs out on Lambert's Castle Hill but the short road walk to Coney's Castle is worth it, particularly in early summer when the bluebells are out. The Five Bells Inn in nearby Whitchurch Canonicorum is dog friendly inside and out.

Axminster is also nearby with a number of good dog friendly pubs and cafés.

Ronnie reckons

Lambert's Castle is a fantastic spot for us dogs, wooded bits to explore and acres of space to run around in. Very good for sociable dogs as you'll probably make lots of new friends. I always enjoy chasing up and down the ramparts of these hillforts! Coney's Castle is fun too, lots more to explore and worth the short bit on the lead along the road.

Coney's Castle.

Lambert's and Coney's Castle are two neighbouring Iron Age hillforts. Dorset is blessed with many of these and almost all offer stunning views and peaceful atmospheres. There are two other hillforts nearby, Pilsdon Pen which is also an excellent dog walking location and Lewesdon Hill. The concentration of these fortifications in this part of Dorset is thought to perhaps relate to the fact that this was border country between the Durotriges tribe that occupied most of Dorset and the Dumnonii of what are now Devon and Cornwall.

From 1709 until 1947 an annual country fair was held on Lambert's Castle Hill in June. This became an important local event and gradually grew in size. In the early nineteenth century an Admiralty Telegraph Station occupied part of the hill, a response to the growing threat of French invasion. Such stations stretched across southern England and used a shutter system to relay messages. The Liberty Trail whose sign you come across marks the route of rebels who, in 1685, joined up with James, Duke of Monmouth in his ill-fated rebellion against James II. Finally, if you can, go to Coney's castle in late spring when a carpet of bluebells covers the ground.

On the Beach!
Some dog friendly beaches where your dog can enjoy a good run around.

There are some wonderful coastal walks in Dorset but I have not included any that make much use of the South West Coast Path because they generally involve cliffs. I never let Ronnie off the lead near a cliff edge; he seems sensible but you never know what's going to distract them. I used to know someone who ran a dog friendly B&B in Swanage and she had quite a number of guests who sadly lost their dogs off the cliffs near Old Harry over the years. Of course, many dogs enjoy a walk on a lead on the coast path but this book features walks where dogs can run free for much of the time. So, given that dogs and people like the coast and seaside, but that many beaches ban dogs for the summer months, I felt it might be useful to suggest some beaches where dogs can run free for most, if not all of the year.

Studland
There are fantastic, sandy beaches at Studland and dogs are welcome all year. However, they must be on a lead 2m or less between 1 May and 30 September. There are various National Trust car parks (see their website) and a café at Knoll Beach (dogs welcome in outside seating). The Bankes Arms is next to the South Beach car park and has a large garden facing the sea, plus dogs arc also welcome inside.

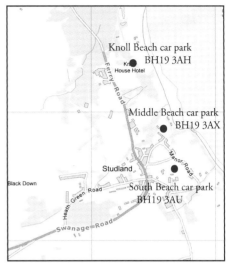

Worbarrow Bay and Tyneham
The deserted village of Tyneham is only open most weekends and school holidays (check on http://www.tyne-hamopc.org.uk/visiting-tyneham/opening-times/). You can walk around the village (dogs best on leads) and also wander down to the sea at Worbarrow Bay where dogs can have a run. All in all it's a good day out for everyone.

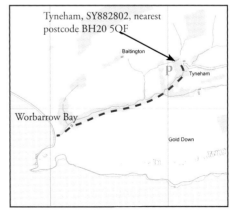

Kimmeridge

Dogs are welcome here all year round. There's plenty of interest on the beach for dogs and humans. The water is shallow and dogs can safely enjoy a paddle or swim. Take care near the cliff by the car park, there's a steep drop. In Kimmeridge village Clavell's Farm Shop and Restaurant welcomes dogs inside and outside.

a relatively quiet, unspoilt spot. There's another parking area (on map) where dogs can run, plus there's a fairly short walk to White Nothe cliff with amazing views over the coast towards Lulworth (see walk 10). Dogs will need to be on a lead for some of this.

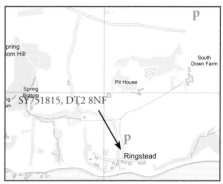

SY751815, DT2 8NF

I found an ammonite!

The view from White Nothe.

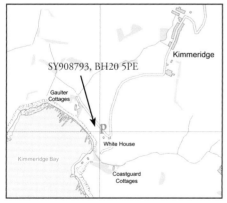

SY908793, BH20 5PE

Ringstead Bay

It's a shingle beach but dogs are welcome all year. There's a car park and café but

Eype

Dogs are welcome all year round on Eype Beach. It's shingle but there's space for a good run.

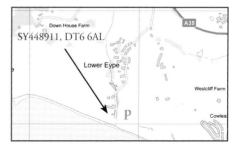

SY448911, DT6 6AL

Charmouth and Lyme Regis

Dogs can run on East Charmouth Beach (east of river mouth) all year. There's plenty of space and humans can try fossil hunting. At Lyme Regis dogs are allowed all year on East Cliff Beach, Church Cliff beach and Monmouth Beach. There's plenty of space on Monmouth Beach, west of The Cobb, and humans can marvel at the amazing ammonite pavement. There are plenty of places to eat and drink that welcome dogs.

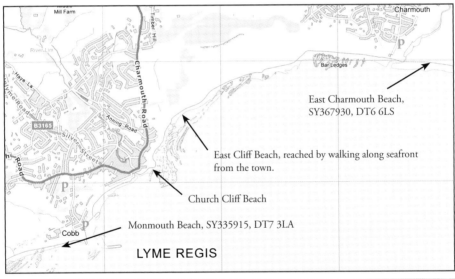

East Charmouth Beach, SY367930, DT6 6LS

East Cliff Beach, reached by walking along seafront from the town.

Church Cliff Beach

Monmouth Beach, SY335915, DT7 3LA

LYME REGIS

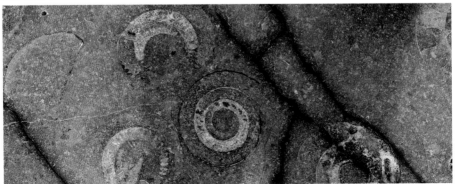

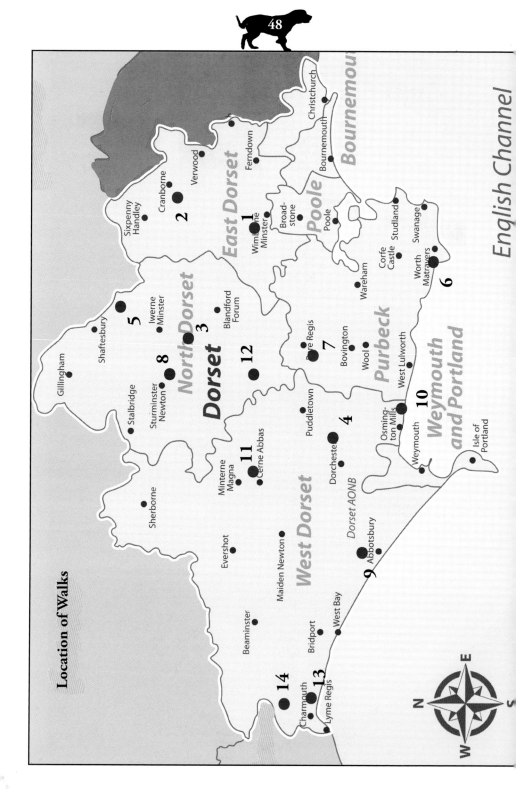

Location of Walks